C000133532

Every Day Matters 2022 Diary

A YEAR OF INSPIRATION
FOR THE MIND, BODY & SPIRIT

Created by
Jess Sharp
as seen on Instagram
@jessrachelsharp

WATKINS
Sharing Wisdom Since 1893

Every Day Matters 2022 Diary

First published in UK and USA in 2021 by
Watkins, an imprint of Watkins Media Limited
89–93 Shepperton Road, London N1 3DF
enquiries@watkinspublishing.co.uk

Copyright © Watkins Media Limited 2021
Text and illustrations © Jess Sharp 2021

Designed by Watkins Media Limited

Illustrator and Author: Jess Sharp
Design: Glen Wilkins
Commissioning Editor: Anya Hayes
Editorial Assistant: Brittany Willis

Desk Diary ISBN: 978-178678-538-1
Pocket Diary ISBN: 978-178678-549-7

All rights reserved. No part of this book may be
reproduced in any form or by any electronic or
mechanical means, including information storage and
retrieval systems, without permission in writing from
the publisher, except by a reviewer who may quote
brief passages in a review.

Colour reproduction by XY Digital, UK
Printed in China

Phases of the Moon:

- ● New moon
- ☽ First quarter
- ○ Full moon
- ☾ Last quarter

Signs of the Zodiac:

♒ Aquarius	January 21–February 19
♓ Pisces	February 20–March 20
♈ Aries	March 21–April 20
♉ Taurus	April 21–May 20
♊ Gemini	May 21–June 21
♋ Cancer	June 22–July 22
♌ Leo	July 23–August 23
♍ Virgo	August 24–September 23
♎ Libra	September 24–October 23
♏ Scorpio	October 24–November 22
♐ Sagittarius	November 23–December 21
♑ Capricorn	December 22–January 20

Abbreviations:

BCE: Before Common Era (equivalent of BC)
CE: Common Era (equivalent of AD)
UK: United Kingdom
SCO: Scotland
NIR: Northern Ireland
ROI: Republic of Ireland
CAN: Canada
USA: United States of America
NZ: New Zealand
AUS: Australia
ACT: Australian Capital Territory
NSW: New South Wales
NT: Northern Territory
QLD: Queensland
SA: South Australia
TAS: Tasmania
VIC: Victoria
WA: Western Australia

Publisher's Notes:

All dates relating to the zodiac signs and the
phases of the moon are based on Greenwich
Mean Time (GMT).

All North American holiday dates are based on
Eastern Standard Time (EST).

Jewish and Islamic holidays begin at sundown on
the date given. Islamic holidays may vary by a
day or two, as the Islamic calendar is based on a
combination of actual sightings of the moon and
astronomical calculations.

Watkins Media Limited cannot accept
responsibility for any injuries or damage
incurred as a result of following the information,
exercises or therapeutic techniques contained in
this book.

Note on Public Holidays:

Holiday dates were correct at the time of going
to press.

2021

JANUARY
```
M  TU  W  TH  F  SA  SU
              1   2   3
4   5   6   7   8   9  10
11  12  13  14  15  16  17
18  19  20  21  22  23  24
25  26  27  28  29  30  31
```

FEBRUARY
```
M  TU  W  TH  F  SA  SU
1   2   3   4   5   6   7
8   9  10  11  12  13  14
15  16  17  18  19  20  21
22  23  24  25  26  27  28
```

MARCH
```
M  TU  W  TH  F  SA  SU
1   2   3   4   5   6   7
8   9  10  11  12  13  14
15  16  17  18  19  20  21
22  23  24  25  26  27  28
29  30  31
```

APRIL
```
M  TU  W  TH  F  SA  SU
                  1   2   3   4
5   6   7   8   9  10  11
12  13  14  15  16  17  18
19  20  21  22  23  24  25
26  27  28  29  30
```

MAY
```
M  TU  W  TH  F  SA  SU
                      1   2
3   4   5   6   7   8   9
10  11  12  13  14  15  16
17  18  19  20  21  22  23
24  25  26  27  28  29  30
31
```

JUNE
```
M  TU  W  TH  F  SA  SU
    1   2   3   4   5   6
7   8   9  10  11  12  13
14  15  16  17  18  19  20
21  22  23  24  25  26  27
28  29  30
```

JULY
```
M  TU  W  TH  F  SA  SU
            1   2   3   4
5   6   7   8   9  10  11
12  13  14  15  16  17  18
19  20  21  22  23  24  25
26  27  28  29  30  31
```

AUGUST
```
M  TU  W  TH  F  SA  SU
                      1
2   3   4   5   6   7   8
9  10  11  12  13  14  15
16  17  18  19  20  21  22
23  24  25  26  27  28  29
30  31
```

SEPTEMBER
```
M  TU  W  TH  F  SA  SU
        1   2   3   4   5
6   7   8   9  10  11  12
13  14  15  16  17  18  19
20  21  22  23  24  25  26
27  28  29  30
```

OCTOBER
```
M  TU  W  TH  F  SA  SU
              1   2   3
4   5   6   7   8   9  10
11  12  13  14  15  16  17
18  19  20  21  22  23  24
25  26  27  28  29  30  31
```

NOVEMBER
```
M  TU  W  TH  F  SA  SU
1   2   3   4   5   6   7
8   9  10  11  12  13  14
15  16  17  18  19  20  21
22  23  24  25  26  27  28
29  30
```

DECEMBER
```
M  TU  W  TH  F  SA  SU
        1   2   3   4   5
6   7   8   9  10  11  12
13  14  15  16  17  18  19
20  21  22  23  24  25  26
27  28  29  30  31
```

2022

JANUARY
```
M  TU  W  TH  F  SA  SU
                      1   2
3   4   5   6   7   8   9
10  11  12  13  14  15  16
17  18  19  20  21  22  23
24  25  26  27  28  29  30
31
```

FEBRUARY
```
M  TU  W  TH  F  SA  SU
    1   2   3   4   5   6
7   8   9  10  11  12  13
14  15  16  17  18  19  20
21  22  23  24  25  26  27
28
```

MARCH
```
M  TU  W  TH  F  SA  SU
    1   2   3   4   5   6
7   8   9  10  11  12  13
14  15  16  17  18  19  20
21  22  23  24  25  26  27
28  29  30  31
```

APRIL
```
M  TU  W  TH  F  SA  SU
                  1   2   3
4   5   6   7   8   9  10
11  12  13  14  15  16  17
18  19  20  21  22  23  24
25  26  27  28  29  30
```

MAY
```
M  TU  W  TH  F  SA  SU
                      1
2   3   4   5   6   7   8
9  10  11  12  13  14  15
16  17  18  19  20  21  22
23  24  25  26  27  28  29
30  31
```

JUNE
```
M  TU  W  TH  F  SA  SU
            1   2   3   4   5
6   7   8   9  10  11  12
13  14  15  16  17  18  19
20  21  22  23  24  25  26
27  28  29  30
```

JULY
```
M  TU  W  TH  F  SA  SU
                  1   2   3
4   5   6   7   8   9  10
11  12  13  14  15  16  17
18  19  20  21  22  23  24
25  26  27  28  29  30  31
```

AUGUST
```
M  TU  W  TH  F  SA  SU
1   2   3   4   5   6   7
8   9  10  11  12  13  14
15  16  17  18  19  20  21
22  23  24  25  26  27  28
29  30  31
```

SEPTEMBER
```
M  TU  W  TH  F  SA  SU
            1   2   3   4
5   6   7   8   9  10  11
12  13  14  15  16  17  18
19  20  21  22  23  24  25
26  27  28  29  30
```

OCTOBER
```
M  TU  W  TH  F  SA  SU
                  1   2
3   4   5   6   7   8   9
10  11  12  13  14  15  16
17  18  19  20  21  22  23
24  25  26  27  28  29  30
31
```

NOVEMBER
```
M  TU  W  TH  F  SA  SU
    1   2   3   4   5   6
7   8   9  10  11  12  13
14  15  16  17  18  19  20
21  22  23  24  25  26  27
28  29  30
```

DECEMBER
```
M  TU  W  TH  F  SA  SU
            1   2   3   4
5   6   7   8   9  10  11
12  13  14  15  16  17  18
19  20  21  22  23  24  25
26  27  28  29  30  31
```

2023

JANUARY
```
M  TU  W  TH  F  SA  SU
                      1
2   3   4   5   6   7   8
9  10  11  12  13  14  15
16  17  18  19  20  21  22
23  24  25  26  27  28  29
30  31
```

FEBRUARY
```
M  TU  W  TH  F  SA  SU
        1   2   3   4   5
6   7   8   9  10  11  12
13  14  15  16  17  18  19
20  21  22  23  24  25  26
27  28
```

MARCH
```
M  TU  W  TH  F  SA  SU
        1   2   3   4   5
6   7   8   9  10  11  12
13  14  15  16  17  18  19
20  21  22  23  24  25  26
27  28  29  30  31
```

APRIL
```
M  TU  W  TH  F  SA  SU
                          1   2
3   4   5   6   7   8   9
10  11  12  13  14  15  16
17  18  19  20  21  22  23
24  25  26  27  28  29  30
```

MAY
```
M  TU  W  TH  F  SA  SU
1   2   3   4   5   6   7
8   9  10  11  12  13  14
15  16  17  18  19  20  21
22  23  24  25  26  27  28
29  30  31
```

JUNE
```
M  TU  W  TH  F  SA  SU
            1   2   3   4
5   6   7   8   9  10  11
12  13  14  15  16  17  18
19  20  21  22  23  24  25
26  27  28  29  30
```

JULY
```
M  TU  W  TH  F  SA  SU
                  1   2
3   4   5   6   7   8   9
10  11  12  13  14  15  16
17  18  19  20  21  22  23
24  25  26  27  28  29  30
31
```

AUGUST
```
M  TU  W  TH  F  SA  SU
    1   2   3   4   5   6
7   8   9  10  11  12  13
14  15  16  17  18  19  20
21  22  23  24  25  26  27
28  29  30  31
```

SEPTEMBER
```
M  TU  W  TH  F  SA  SU
              1   2   3
4   5   6   7   8   9  10
11  12  13  14  15  16  17
18  19  20  21  22  23  24
25  26  27  28  29  30
```

OCTOBER
```
M  TU  W  TH  F  SA  SU
                      1
2   3   4   5   6   7   8
9  10  11  12  13  14  15
16  17  18  19  20  21  22
23  24  25  26  27  28  29
30  31
```

NOVEMBER
```
M  TU  W  TH  F  SA  SU
        1   2   3   4   5
6   7   8   9  10  11  12
13  14  15  16  17  18  19
20  21  22  23  24  25  26
27  28  29  30
```

DECEMBER
```
M  TU  W  TH  F  SA  SU
              1   2   3
4   5   6   7   8   9  10
11  12  13  14  15  16  17
18  19  20  21  22  23  24
25  26  27  28  29  30  31
```

Argentina	Jan 1, Feb 28–Mar 1, Mar 24, Apr 2, Apr 14–15, May 1, May 25, Jun 17, Jun 20, Jul 9, Aug 15, Oct 10, Nov 21, Dec 8, Dec 25
Australia	Jan 1, Jan 3, Jan 26, Feb 14 (TAS), Mar 7 (WA), Mar 14 (ACT, SA, TAS, VIC), Mar 21, Apr 15, Apr 16 (exc TAS, WA), Apr 17–18, Apr 25, May 2 (NT, QLD), May 30 (ACT), Jun 6 (WA), Jun 13 (exc QLD, WA), Aug 1 (NSW, NT), Aug 10 (QLD), Sep 26 (WA), Sep 30 (VIC), Oct 3 (ACT, NSW, QLD, SA), Nov 1 (VIC), Nov 7 (TAS), Nov 11, Dec 24 (NT, QLD, SA), Dec 25, Dec 26, Dec 31 (NT, SA)
Austria	Jan 1, Jan 6, Apr 18, May 1, May 26, Jun 6, Jun 16, Aug 15, Oct 5, Oct 26, Nov 1, Dec 8, Dec 25–26
Belgium	Jan 1, Apr 15, Apr 17–18, May 1, May 26–27, Jun 5–6, Jul 21, Aug 15, Nov 1, Nov 11, Dec 25–26
Brazil	Jan 1, Apr 15, Apr 21, May 1, Sep 7, Oct 12, Nov 2, Nov 15, Dec 25
Canada	Jan 1, Jan 3, Apr 15, Apr 18, May 23, Jul 1, Aug 1, Sep 5, Oct 10, Nov 11, Dec 25-26
China	Jan 1, Jan 31, Feb 1, Feb 2–6, Mar 8, Apr 5, May 1, May 4, Jun 1, Jun 3, Aug 1, Sep 10, Oct 1–7
Denmark	Jan 1, Apr 14–15, Apr 17–18, May 13, May 26, Jun 5–6, Dec 25–26
Finland	Jan 1, Jan 6, Apr 15, Apr 18, May 1, May 26, Jun 5, Jun 24–25, Nov 5, Dec 6, Dec 24–26
France	Jan 1, Apr 18, May 1, May 8, May 26, Jun 6, Jul 14, Aug 15, Nov 1, Nov 11, Dec 25
Germany	Jan 1, Apr 15, Apr 18, May 1, May 26, Jun 6, Oct 3, Dec 25–26, Dec 31
Greece	Jan 1, Jan 6, Mar 7, Mar 25, Apr 22, Apr 25, May 1, Jun 13, Aug 15, Oct 28, Dec 25–26
India	Jan 26, May 3, Aug 15, Oct 2, Dec 25
Indonesia	Jan 1, Feb 1, Mar 1, Apr 15, May 1, May 3–4, May 26, Jun 1, Jul 10, July 30, Aug 17, Oct 8, Oct 24, Dec 25
Israel	Apr 16, Apr 22, May 5, May 29, Jun 5, Sep 26–27, Oct 5, Oct 10, Oct 17
Italy	Jan 1, Jan 6, Apr 18, Apr 25, May 1, Jun 2, Aug 15, Nov 1, Dec 8, Dec 25–26
Japan	Jan 1–3, Jan 10, Feb 11, Feb 23, Mar 21, Apr 29, May 3–5, Jul 18, Aug 11, Sep 19, Sept 23, Oct 10, Nov 3, Nov 23, dec 25, Dec 31

Luxembourg	Jan 1, Apr 15, Apr 18, May 1, May 9, May 26, Jun 6, Jun 23, Aug 15, Nov 1, Dec 24–26
Mexico	Jan 1, Feb 5, Feb 7, Mar 21, Apr 14–15, May 1, Sep 16, Nov 20–21, Dec 12, Dec 25
Netherlands	Jan 1, Apr 15, Apr 17–18, Apr 27, May 26, June 5–6, Dec 25–26
New Zealand	Jan 1, Jan 3–4, Feb 6–7, Apr 15, Apr 18, Apr 25, Jun 6, Oct 24, Dec 25–27
Nigeria	Jan 1, Apr 15, Apr 18, May 1, May 3–4, Jun 12, Jul 10–11, Oct 1, Oct 8, Dec 25–26
Pakistan	Feb 5, Mar 23, May 1, May 3–5, Jul 10–11, Aug 8–9, Aug 14, Oct 9, Dec 25
Poland	Jan 1, Jan 6, Apr 17–18, May 1, May 3, Jun 5, Jun 16, Aug 15, Nov 1, Nov 11, Dec 25–26
Portugal	Jan 1, Apr 15, Apr 17, Apr 25, May 1, Jun 10, Aug 15, Oct 5, Nov 1, Dec 1, Dec 8, Dec 25
Republic of Ireland	Jan 1, Mar 17, Apr 18, May 2, Jun 6, Aug 1, Oct 31, Dec 25–26
Russia	Jan 1, Jan 3-6, Jan 7, Feb 23, Mar 8, May 1–2, May 9, Jun 12–13, Nov 4
South Africa	Jan 1, Mar 21, Apr 15, Apr 18, Apr 27, May 1–2, Jun 16, Aug 9, Sep 24, Dec 16, Dec 25–26
Spain	Jan 1, Jan 6, Apr 15, May 1–2, Aug 15, Oct 12, Nov 1, Dec 6, Dec 8, Dec 25
Sweden	Jan 1, Jan 6, Apr 15–18, May 1, May 26, June 4–6, Jun 24–25, Nov 5, Dec 24–26, Dec 31
Turkey	Jan 1, Apr 23, May 1, May 3–5, May 19, Jul 10–13, Jul 15, Aug 30, Oct 29
United Kingdom	Jan 1, Jan 3, Jan 4 (SCO), Mar 17 (NIR), Apr 15, Apr 18, May 2, Jun 2–3, Jul 12 (NIR), Aug 1 (SCO), Aug 29 (exc SCO), Nov 30 (SCO), Dec 25–27
United States	Jan 1, Jan 17, Feb 21, May 30, Jul 4, Sep 5, Oct 10, Nov 11, Nov 24, Dec 25–26, Dec 31

WELCOME TO 2022!

Hello! Welcome to a new year brimming with empowering and exciting adventures.

The beginning of a new year can feel a little overwhelming. As December turns to January, we are often bombarded with messaging that tries to convince us that we need to change; that tells us how we should strive to be "better" and offers myriad solutions for leaving behind our old ways to replace them with something allegedly more perfect.

Well, here's the thing. I don't believe in "new year, new you". I believe in growth and self-compassion. A new year is a time for reflection and review, yes – but it is mostly a time to leap into the present with renewed vigour for who we already are. There should be no negative self-talk, no self-destructive goals, no thinking we have to chase an impossible version of ourselves.

Over the coming months, I'll guide you through 12 themes to help you explore and reflect on your emotional self and your physical and mental wellbeing. On every page of this diary, there are illustrations and prompts, and space for your own observations about how you feel. All these tools are aimed at helping you to navigate the year in the most positive ways possible.

So here's to a year of compassion, kindness, self-exploration and growth. I hope it is a year of fulfilment and happiness.

GRATITUDE

Gratitude is a wonderful way to reframe our thinking. Day-to-day life is busy and often messy and it's all too easy to get caught up in the repetitive speed of it all. Pausing to practise gratitude can help us to re-align our priorities and remind us of what is most important and fulfilling.

Just as sunflowers grow up to seek the sun, we should always be aware of the goodness in life that we need in order to continue growing happily and healthily. This goodness is so unique and will differ from person to person. Gratitude strips this back for us, helping to clarify what makes our own soul sing.

Use the prompts over the coming weeks to help you find and practise gratitude in your day-to-day life.

AFFIRMATION OF THE MONTH

I am so grateful to be here. Embracing all I have and all I am

DEC 27 – JAN 2

gratitude

27 / MONDAY ☾

28 / TUESDAY

29 / WEDNESDAY

NOTES

> "Be happy in the moment, that's enough.
> Each moment is all we need, not more"

MOTHER TERESA (1910–1997), CATHOLIC MISSIONARY

30 / THURSDAY

31 / FRIDAY
New Year's Eve

1 / SATURDAY
New Year's Day
Kwanzaa ends

2 / SUNDAY ●

LOOK HOW FAR YOU HAVE COME

Sometimes we get swept up in the pace of life, never really stopping to take note of how far we've come. Take a moment to think about something you have that you are grateful for now but didn't have a year ago. Make a list of things you've changed. You've probably accomplished more than you realize.

JAN 3 – JAN 9
gratitude

3 / MONDAY
New Year's Day
(substitute day)

_____
_____
_____
_____
_____
_____
_____
_____
_____
_____
_____
_____

4 / TUESDAY
Public Holiday (SCO, NZ)

_____
_____
_____
_____
_____
_____
_____
_____
_____
_____
_____
_____

5 / WEDNESDAY

_____
_____
_____
_____
_____
_____
_____
_____
_____
_____
_____
_____

NOTES

_____
_____
_____

> ## "Gratitude is not only the greatest of virtues, but the parent of all others"
>
> MARCUS TULLIUS CICERO (106–43BCE), ROMAN PHILOSOPHER

6 / THURSDAY
Epiphany

7 / FRIDAY
Christmas Day (Orthodox)

8 / SATURDAY

9 / SUNDAY ☽

THE ART OF COMFORT

Art/music/books can be a wonderful comfort in life and provide much-needed inspiration and solace. Which artist, musician or author are you grateful for? Spend time this week indulging yourself in their work. Whether it be a trip to an a gallery, reading a much-loved book or listening to your favourite song on a walk in the sunshine.

JAN 10 – JAN 16
gratitude

10 / MONDAY

11 / TUESDAY

12 / WEDNESDAY

NOTES

> "I love my past. I love my present. I'm not ashamed of what I've had, and I'm not sad because I have it no longer"

SIDONIE-GABRIELLE COLETTE (1873–1954), FRENCH NOVELIST

13 / THURSDAY

14 / FRIDAY
New Year's Day (Orthodox)

15 / SATURDAY

16 / SUNDAY

GRATEFUL FOR YOU

Often, we can take for granted the wonderful people in our life. Take a moment to think of someone special that you are grateful for and write down that person's good qualities and the things that you love about them. If you feel comfortable you could always show them too; it may give them a much-needed boost!

JAN 17 – JAN 23

gratitude

17 / MONDAY ○
Martin Luther King, Jr. Day

18 / TUESDAY

19 / WEDNESDAY

NOTES

> ## "The highest tribute to the dead is not grief but gratitude"
>
> THORNTON WILDER (1897–1975), AMERICAN PLAYWRIGHT

20 / THURSDAY

21 / FRIDAY ≈

22 / SATURDAY

_____
_____
_____
_____
_____

23 / SUNDAY

_____
_____
_____
_____
_____

GOLDEN MEMORIES

Memories are often a comfort, reminding us of past cherished moments. Think of a particular memory you have and why it makes you so happy. Do you have any mementos anchored to it – trinkets, photos, smells? Spend an hour or so sitting and going through them and really soak them up.

JAN 24 – JAN 30
gratitude

24 / MONDAY

25 / TUESDAY ☾
Burns Night (SCO)

26 / WEDNESDAY
Australia Day

NOTES

"Do not spoil what you have by desiring what you have not"

EPICURUS (*c.* 341–270BCE), ANCIENT GREEK PHILOSOPHER

27 / THURSDAY
International Holocaust
Remembrance Day

_____

_____

_____

_____

_____

_____

_____

_____

_____

_____

28 / FRIDAY

_____

_____

_____

_____

_____

_____

_____

_____

_____

_____

29 / SATURDAY

_____

_____

_____

_____

30 / SUNDAY

_____

_____

_____

_____

A LIGHT IN THE DARKNESS

Sometimes the most difficult times can teach
us important truths. Finding gratitude within
challenge is incredibly difficult, but practising
gratitude here can offer us pieces of self-
discovery. Has that colleague at work who you
don't quite click with taught you empathy and
patience? Can you be grateful for this growth?

JANUARY OVERVIEW

M	TU	W	TH	F	SA	SU
27	28	29	30	31	1	2
3	4	5	6	7	8	9
10	11	12	13	14	15	16
17	18	19	20	21	22	23
24	25	26	27	28	29	30
31	1	2	3	4	5	6

this month I am grateful for . . .

_____

_____

_____

_____

_____

_____

REFLECTIONS ON GRATITUDE

In what areas of your life have you discovered a newfound sense of gratitude for this month?

_____

_____

_____

_____

_____

How did it feel to focus more on what you are grateful for?

_____

_____

_____

_____

_____

Do you think practising gratitude could help you as the year unfolds? How and why?

_____

_____

_____

_____

FEBRUARY

BRAVERY

To show bravery is often seen as a big, bold move of facing something scary. Of course this can be true, but bravery isn't always big gestures and boldness. Sometimes it's quiet and unseen, but still very much there.

It's getting out of bed when your heart feels too heavy to even move. It's driving to a friend's house when you have to use the motorway you hate travelling on. It's making the phone call that scares you.

Bravery is both big and small, loud and quiet. It is relative to our own troubles and experiences and every act of bravery deserves recognition and celebration.

Fill in each activity for this month to help you find and celebrate your own personal bravery.

AFFIRMATION OF THE MONTH

I acknowledge that my bravery will look different each day, and that is more than enough

JAN 31 – FEB 6
Bravery

31 / MONDAY

1 / TUESDAY ●
St Brigid's Day (Imbolc)
Black History Month begins
(CAN, USA)
Chinese New Year (Year of
the Tiger)

2 / WEDNESDAY
Candlemas
Groundhog Day

NOTES

> ## "Courage is the ladder on which all the other virtues mount"
>
> CLARE BOOTHE LUCE (1903–1987), AMERICAN POLITICIAN

3 / THURSDAY

4 / FRIDAY

5 / SATURDAY

6 / SUNDAY
Waitangi Day

FIND YOUR COURAGE

When we fear something, it often becomes bigger and bigger the more we think about it. When we are not feeling our bravest, we tend to put off the scary things. Think of one thing in particular that you've been putting off. Can you find a little bit of bravery at some point this week to tackle it and get it off your mind?

FEB 7 – FEB 13

Bravery

7 / MONDAY
Waitangi Day observed

8 / TUESDAY ☽

9 / WEDNESDAY

NOTES

> ## "The most difficult thing is the decision to act, the rest is merely tenacity"
>
> AMELIA EARHART (1897–1937), AMERICAN AVIATOR

10 / THURSDAY

---

11 / FRIDAY

---

12 / SATURDAY
Abraham Lincoln's birthday

---

13 / SUNDAY

YOU ARE SO MUCH BRAVER THAN YOU THINK

We recognize bravery in others more, as we are our own worst critics. Who do you see as brave, and why? Think about what qualities they possess. Do you perhaps have some of them too? Write them down and allow yourself to feel how they have positively affected your life.

FEB 14 – FEB 20
Bravery

14 / MONDAY
St Valentine's Day

15 / TUESDAY
Nirvana Day

16 / WEDNESDAY ○

NOTES

> ## "Courage is resistance to fear, mastery of fear – not absence of fear"
>
> MARK TWAIN (1835–1910), AMERICAN AUTHOR

17 / THURSDAY

18 / FRIDAY

19 / SATURDAY

20 / SUNDAY ♓

STRONG, CAPABLE AND BRAVE

Throughout our lives we face various challenges that require bravery. As we tackle them and they pass, it's easy to forget what we have faced and achieved. Write down times in the past when you have shown bravery. Use these as a reminder that you are capable of being brave – even when you do not feel it.

FEB 21 – FEB 27
Bravery

21 / MONDAY
Presidents' Day

22 / TUESDAY

23 / WEDNESDAY ☾

NOTES

> ## "You don't have to see the whole staircase – just take the first step"
>
> MARTIN LUTHER KING JR. (1929–1968), AMERICAN ACTIVIST

24 / THURSDAY

25 / FRIDAY

26 / SATURDAY

27 / SUNDAY

DEAR FEARS

Sometimes our fears build up and become a looming shadow over our lives. If they were a person, constantly making you feel intimidated, what would you say to them? Try writing them a letter, explaining how they are affecting you. Remember that you are strong, resilient and more than capable of challenging them.

FEBRUARY OVERVIEW

M	TU	W	TH	F	SA	SU
31	1	2	3	4	5	6
7	8	9	10	11	12	13
14	15	16	17	18	19	20
21	22	23	24	25	26	27
28	1	2	3	4	5	6

This month I am grateful for . . .

_____

_____

_____

_____

_____

_____

REFLECTIONS ON BRAVERY

In what ways have you recognized your own bravery this month?

How did it feel to unpack what bravery feels like and entails for you?

Are there any ways you'd like to develop your bravery in the future?

MARCH

RESILIENCE

Resilience is not simply carrying on through hard times as if nothing has happened, or refusing to show any emotion. Resilience is about trying again. It's about feeling how you feel, acknowledging it and reminding yourself that you've faced similar hills and heartaches before and can face and get through them again. It's about learning from past experiences and trusting that you have what it takes to get through new ones, even when it really doesn't feel like it. Resilience is deep strength and an unwavering belief that, even when you're feeling your weakest, you will get through it and you will be okay.

AFFIRMATION OF THE MONTH

I am more resilient than I think and so much stronger than I feel

FEB 28 – MAR 6

Resilience

28 / MONDAY

1 / TUESDAY
St David's Day
Shrove Tuesday

2 / WEDNESDAY ●
Ash Wednesday

NOTES

> "Never give up, for that is just the place and time that the tide will turn"

HARRIET BEECHER STOWE (1811–1896), AMERICAN AUTHOR

3 / THURSDAY
Losar (Tibetan New Year)
World Book Day

4 / FRIDAY

5 / SATURDAY

6 / SUNDAY

THE COMFORT OF ROUTINE

When times are tough, routine can be a saving grace and give us a sense of normality. Think about your morning. Do you have a set routine? Are there any changes you could make to enhance your energy, calm and positivity? Try creating a new routine this month. Notice how it makes you feel.

MAR 7 – MAR 13

ReSiLieNce

7 / MONDAY
Labour Day (WA)

8 / TUESDAY
International Women's Day

9 / WEDNESDAY

NOTES

"It's easier to go down a hill than up it, but the view is much better at the top"

HENRY WARD BEECHER (1813–1887), AMERICAN CLERGYMAN AND SPEAKER

10 / THURSDAY ☾

11 / FRIDAY

12 / SATURDAY

13 / SUNDAY
Daylight Saving Time starts (CAN, USA)

YOU GOT THROUGH IT

Every time you have overcome a crisis, you have exercised resilience. No matter how you got through it, your resilience has been paramount in guiding you – even if you didn't feel it in the moment. Think of a time when you were struggling, and commend yourself for getting through it. You are allowed to feel proud.

MAR 14 – MAR 20
Resilience

14 / MONDAY
Commonwealth Day
Public Holiday (ACT, SA,
TAS, VIC)

15 / TUESDAY

16 / WEDNESDAY
Purim begins at sundown

NOTES

> ## "The best way to treat obstacles is to use them as stepping stones"
>
> ENID BLYTON (1897–1968), ENGLISH AUTHOR

17 / THURSDAY
St Patrick's Day

18 / FRIDAY ○
Holi (Festival of Colours)

19 / SATURDAY

20 / SUNDAY
Spring Equinox (UK, ROI, CAN, USA)
Autumn Equinox (AUS, NZ)

SELF-CARE IS NOT SELFISH

Life can be draining, and we need to remember to take care of ourselves. Self-care recharges us, helping us handle all that life throws at us. Take some time this week just for you. Whether it be a walk in nature, a solo coffee break or a therapy session. It is important to allocate yourself time to refill your own resources.

MAR 21 – MAR 27
ResiLience

21 / MONDAY ♈

22 / TUESDAY

23 / WEDNESDAY

NOTES

> ## "Rivers know this: there is no hurry. We shall get there someday"
>
> A.A. MILNE (1882–1956), ENGLISH AUTHOR

24 / THURSDAY

25 / FRIDAY ☾

26 / SATURDAY

27 / SUNDAY
Mother's Day (UK)
British Summer Time Begins

GOING THROUGH CHANGES

Change is an inevitable part of life and to embrace it requires resilience. How do you cope with change? Think about the last big change you encountered. How did you feel, and react, what did you learn? Knowing what helped, and what didn't, will prepare you for moving through the next challenge.

MARCH OVERVIEW

M	TU	W	TH	F	SA	SU
28	1	2	3	4	5	6
7	8	9	10	11	12	13
14	15	16	17	18	19	20
21	22	23	24	25	26	27
28	29	30	31	1	2	3

This month I am grateful for . . .

_____

_____

_____

_____

_____

_____

_____

REFLECTIONS ON RESILIENCE

In what ways have you acknowledged your own resilience this month?

_____

_____

_____

_____

_____

How did it feel to think about resilience and what that looks like for you?

_____

_____

_____

_____

_____

Do you think being able to recognize your own resilience might help you feel more prepared for future ups and downs?

_____

_____

_____

_____

_____

COMPASSION

Compassion is a light in the darkness. A steadying hand when your ground is uncertain. It is understanding that someone else is hurting and holding space for that.

Compassion can be difficult to implement at times; it is easy to be separated from other people. To practise compassion – to extend feelings of sympathy and to want to protect someone from their suffering – can help you obtain a deeper level of understanding of someone else's experience. This can often help you to achieve a deeper level of inner peace.

Follow the weekly prompts for this month to help you practise compassion for others and – equally as important – for yourself.

AFFIRMATION OF THE MONTH

I am worthy of the compassion I so freely give to others

MAR 28 – APR 3

compassion

28 / MONDAY	29 / TUESDAY	30 / WEDNESDAY

NOTES

> "If you want others to be happy, practise compassion. If you want to be happy, practise compassion"
>
> 14TH DALAI LAMA (1935–PRESENT), BUDDHIST MONK

31 / THURSDAY
April Fools' Day

1 / FRIDAY ●

2 / SATURDAY
Ramadan begins at sundown

_____
_____
_____
_____
_____

3 / SUNDAY

_____
_____
_____
_____

YOUR NEEDS ARE IMPORTANT

Compassion is often much easier to give to others than to yourself, but you are equally as worthy of receiving it. This week think of something you're being hard on yourself for, then actively remind yourself of this: "I deserve the love and compassion I give to others. I deserve empathy. I deserve forgiveness."

APR 4 – APR 10

compassion

4 / MONDAY	5 / TUESDAY	6 / WEDNESDAY

NOTES

> "The greatest good you can do for
> another is not just to share your riches,
> but to reveal to him his own"

BENJAMIN DISRAELI (1804–1881), FORMER BRITISH PRIME MINISTER

7 / THURSDAY

8 / FRIDAY

9 / SATURDAY ☽

10 / SUNDAY
Palm Sunday

MORE COMPASSION, MORE CONNECTION

Emotions can sometimes be overwhelming in times of stress or confrontation. This week, when confronted with anger or frustration, try to find the strength to practise more compassion. Take note to see if it leads to a different dynamic or a deeper level of connection with them.

APR 11 – APR 17

compassion

11 / MONDAY	12 / TUESDAY	13 / WEDNESDAY

NOTES

> "If your compassion does not include yourself, it is incomplete"

GAUTAMA BUDDHA (c. 563–483BCE), FOUNDER OF BUDDHISM

14 / THURSDAY
Maundy Thursday

_____
_____
_____
_____
_____
_____
_____
_____
_____
_____
_____

15 / FRIDAY
Good Friday
Passover begins at sundown
Vesaak Day (Buddha Day)

_____
_____
_____
_____
_____

16 / SATURDAY ○

_____
_____
_____
_____

17 / SUNDAY
Easter Sunday

_____
_____
_____
_____
_____

A HELPING HAND

Compassion can change another person's world; it can make them feel seen and loved. Think of someone in your life right now who deserves to feel seen. Do something special so they know you're there. This could be as simple as a nice text message, or sending flowers or a package of their favourite comfort food.

APR 18 – APR 24

compassion

18 / MONDAY
Easter Monday

19 / TUESDAY

20 / WEDNESDAY

NOTES

> "Love is all we have, the only way that each can help the other"
>
> EURIPIDES (c. 480–406BCE), GREEK DRAMATIST

21 / THURSDAY ♉

22 / FRIDAY
Earth Day

23 / SATURDAY ☾
Passover ends at sundown
St George's Day

24 / SUNDAY
Easter Sunday (Orthodox)

WORK HARD, RELAX HARD

We live in a society that values hustle, where working hard is seen as a positive trait. If you're not working hard, you're deemed lazy. This just isn't true. This week, allow yourself to rest and remind yourself not to feel guilty. You are more than deserving of some time away from the daily grind. Give yourself permission to pause.

APR 25 – MAY 1

compassion

25 / MONDAY
Anzac Day

26 / TUESDAY

27 / WEDNESDAY

NOTES

> ## "Compassion is the radicalism of our time"
> 14TH DALAI LAMA (1935–PRESENT), BUDDHIST MONK

28 / THURSDAY

29 / FRIDAY

30 / SATURDAY ●

1 / SUNDAY
Beltane

LESS COMPARISON, MORE COMPASSION

It's too easy to get caught up in the comparison trap, constantly looking to others and berating yourself for not having what they have. Show some self-compassion and stop falling down these negative rabbit holes. Remind yourself that we are all on our own personal journeys.

APRIL OVERVIEW

M	TU	W	TH	F	SA	SU
28	29	30	31	1	2	3
4	5	6	7	8	9	10
11	12	13	14	15	16	17
18	19	20	21	22	23	24
25	26	27	28	29	30	1

this month I am grateful for . . .

_____

_____

_____

_____

_____

_____

REFLECTIONS ON COMPASSION

In what ways have you shown yourself compassion this month?

_____

_____

_____

_____

_____

How does it feel when other people show you compassion? Does it alter how you feel about yourself?

_____

_____

_____

_____

_____

How can you continue to show more compassion for yourself and for others in the future?

_____

_____

_____

_____

_____

MAY

GROWTH

Emotional growth is something that happens when we often don't realize or notice. Every experience we encounter shapes us. Every experience sets up how we deal with the next; good or bad. Whether we realize it or not, we are always learning, and if we are not, we usually repeat mistakes until we do.

Growth isn't always easy, but often the most difficult periods teach us the most. Painful and uncomfortable as these times are, the positive is that we can always learn and grow from them.

Much like a plant needs sunshine and rain equally to thrive, so do we. As long as we trust in our own journey and remind ourselves that the path is guiding us somewhere worth going, the growing pains can seem a little more bearable.

AFFIRMATION OF THE MONTH

I am always growing
and learning

MAY 2 – MAY 8

growth

2 / MONDAY
May Day (NT, QLD)
Early May Bank Holiday
(UK, ROI)
Ramadan ends at sundown
(Eid al-Fitr)

3 / TUESDAY

4 / WEDNESDAY

NOTES

> "Very early, I knew that the only object in life was to grow"

MARGARET FULLER (1810–1850), AMERICAN JOURNALIST

5 / THURSDAY
Cinco de Mayo

_____
_____
_____
_____
_____
_____
_____
_____
_____

6 / FRIDAY

_____
_____
_____
_____
_____
_____
_____
_____
_____

7 / SATURDAY

_____
_____
_____
_____

8 / SUNDAY
Mother's Day (CAN, USA, AUS, NZ)

_____
_____
_____
_____

WHAT I KNOW TO BE TRUE

Growth is an ongoing process and we can lose sight of the growing we've already done. Take a moment to pause and think about something you are certain of today that you were uncertain of a year ago. Did you leave a job that was making you unhappy? Move cities? Recognize that growth, and celebrate it!

MAY 9 – MAY 15

Growth

9 / MONDAY ☽

_____
_____
_____
_____
_____
_____
_____
_____
_____
_____
_____
_____

10 / TUESDAY

_____
_____
_____
_____
_____
_____
_____
_____
_____
_____
_____
_____

11 / WEDNESDAY

_____
_____
_____
_____
_____
_____
_____
_____
_____
_____
_____
_____

NOTES

_____
_____
_____
_____

> ## "All growth is a leap in the dark"
> HENRY MILLER (1891–1980), AMERICAN WRITER

12 / THURSDAY

----

13 / FRIDAY

----

14 / SATURDAY

----

15 / SUNDAY
Vesak Day (Buddha Day)

LETTER TO YOUR YOUNGER SELF

Growing up is messy and difficult and we are often too hard on ourselves. Take a moment this week to turn to the "Inspired Journalling" section at the back of the diary. Once there, pick a significant age and write a letter of support to that past version of yourself. Let them know that the growing pains are worth it.

MAY 16 – MAY 22

growth

16 / MONDAY ○

17 / TUESDAY

18 / WEDNESDAY

NOTES

> "From a small seed a mighty trunk may grow"

AESCHYLUS (c. 525–c. 456), GREEK PLAYWRIGHT

19 / THURSDAY

20 / FRIDAY

21 / SATURDAY ♊

22 / SUNDAY ☾

NOURISH THE GOOD THOUGHTS AND LET THEM GROW

Negative self-talk can feel like a barrier to growth. Self-belief and self-love are so difficult to practise at times, but are essential to how we feel and carry ourselves through life. Next time you hear that negative internal voice, tell yourself that this is an opinion not a fact.

MAY 23 – MAY 29

Growth

23 / MONDAY
Victoria Day (CAN, except NS, QC)

24 / TUESDAY

25 / WEDNESDAY

NOTES

> "If we don't change, we don't grow. If we don't grow, we aren't really living"
>
> GAIL SHEELY (1937–2020), AMERICAN WRITER

26 / THURSDAY
Ascension Day

_____

_____

_____

_____

_____

_____

_____

_____

27 / FRIDAY

_____

_____

_____

_____

_____

_____

_____

_____

28 / SATURDAY

_____

_____

_____

29 / SUNDAY

_____

_____

_____

_____

SOMETHING NEW

Experiencing new places, people and things can be a wonderful way to expand our minds and push out of our comfort zone. This week, try to immerse youself into something new. Whether it be a new place, genre of book or film, even a conversation with someone new. Has it inspired you or altered your habitual view on things?

MAY OVERVIEW

M	TU	W	TH	F	SA	SU
25	26	27	28	29	30	1
2	3	4	5	6	7	8
9	10	11	12	13	14	15
16	17	18	19	20	21	22
23	24	25	26	27	28	29
30	31	1	2	3	4	5

this month I am grateful for . . .

_____

_____

_____

_____

_____

_____

REFLECTIONS ON GROWTH

Has thinking about growth led you to recognize more about yourself and acknowledge anything you haven't thought about before?

_____

_____

_____

_____

_____

Do you think you have grown over the past month? How?

_____

_____

_____

_____

_____

In what ways will you seek out opportunities for growth in the future?

_____

_____

_____

_____

_____

SIMPLICITY

This world can be a noisy, busy place that often feels like a continual treadmill of task after task, goal after goal. It's important in amongst the hustle and bustle that we allow ourselves to find comfort in simplicity. Whether that be taking a scenic route home and stopping to feel the warmth of the sun on your skin, or having a cup of tea with a friend. There is beauty to be found in the simple things, in finding moments of natural calm in a hectic, tangled world.

You do not always have to be striving for more, or continually reaching for the next milestone. Sometimes moving forwards can actually be feeling content with the simplicity of standing still, and soaking that in for a while.

AFFIRMATION OF THE MONTH

I will remember that the small, simple moments are not small at all

MAY 30 – JUN 5

simplicity

30 / MONDAY ●
Memorial Day (USA)

31 / TUESDAY

1 / WEDNESDAY

NOTES

> ## "Remember that very little is needed to make a happy life"
>
> MARCUS AURELIUS (121–180AD), ROMAN EMPEROR

2 / THURSDAY
Spring Bank Holiday (UK)

3 / FRIDAY
Platinum Jubilee Bank
Holiday (UK)

4 / SATURDAY

5 / SUNDAY
Pentecost (Whit Sunday)

THE IMPORTANCE OF BALANCE

When our lives are hectic, we forget to
prioritize the important things. Think about
the last 24 hours. How much time have you
spent doing what you have to do, rather than
what you want to do? What commitments
drain you? Could you simplify, to allow yourself
more time for moments you can cherish?

JUN 6 – JUN 12

simplicity

6 / MONDAY
June Bank Holiday (ROI)
Queen's birthday celebrated
(NZ)
Western Australia Day (WA)

7 / TUESDAY ☽

8 / WEDNESDAY

NOTES

> "I am beginning to learn that it is the sweet, simple things of life which are the real ones after all"

LAURA INGALLS WILDER (1867–1957), AMERICAN WRITER

9 / THURSDAY

_____

_____

_____

_____

_____

_____

_____

_____

_____

_____

10 / FRIDAY

_____

_____

_____

_____

_____

_____

_____

_____

_____

11 / SATURDAY

_____

_____

_____

_____

12 / SUNDAY

_____

_____

_____

_____

CLEAR LIVING SPACE, CLEAR MIND

Are you a clutter lover, or do you prefer a more stripped back way of living? If you fall more on the clutter side, spend a little bit of this week tackling a space in your home and simplifying it. Whether it is a room, a cupboard, wardrobe or a kitchen drawer, give it a good once over and get rid of all you no longer need.

JUN 13 – JUN 19

simplicity

13 / MONDAY
Queen's birthday celebrated
(AUS, except QLD, WA)

14 / TUESDAY ○

15 / WEDNESDAY

NOTES

"Beware the barrenness of a busy life"

SOCRATES (c. 470–399BCE), GREEK PHILOSOPHER

16 / THURSDAY

17 / FRIDAY

18 / SATURDAY

_____

19 / SUNDAY
Father's Day (UK, ROI, CAN, USA)

SIMPLE PLEASURES

Pleasures are what make life worthwhile. They do not have to be big or grand; all they have to do is warm our souls. Think about one thing that brings you pleasure. Whether it's spending time with a loved one or enjoying a hot drink on a cold evening. This week, make time to indulge yourself with that simple pleasure.

JUN 20 – JUN 26

simplicity

20 / MONDAY

21 / TUESDAY ☾
Summer Solstice (UK, ROI, CAN, USA)
Winter Solstice (US, NZ)

22 / WEDNESDAY ♋

NOTES

> "Receive with simplicity everything that happens to you"
>
> RASHI (1040–1105), FRENCH RABBI

23 / THURSDAY

----

24 / FRIDAY

----

25 / SATURDAY

----

26 / SUNDAY

SAY NO MORE

Saying no can be so hard, especially if by nature you're a people pleaser. This week, try to implement a boundary and say no to something you do not want or have to do. No is a completely okay answer to give, and can still be done kindly. Sometimes we need to say no to others in order to say yes to ourselves.

JUNE OVERVIEW

M	TU	W	TH	F	SA	SU
30	31	1	2	3	4	5
6	7	8	9	10	11	12
13	14	15	16	17	18	19
20	21	22	23	24	25	26
27	28	29	30	1	2	3

This month I am grateful for . . .

_____

_____

_____

_____

_____

_____

REFLECTIONS ON SIMPLICITY

Has stripping back and thinking about the simple things been beneficial?

_____

_____

_____

_____

_____

How has concentrating on the little things felt?

_____

_____

_____

_____

In what ways can you implement simplicity positively into your future?

_____

_____

_____

_____

JULY

MINDFULNESS

Every day, our minds are constantly whirring busily, never fully switching off from persistent notifications, sources of information, ever-piling worries and never-ending to-do lists. Often we forget to connect with our sensations and inner space – mindfulness asks us to pause and hone in on the sights, sounds, tastes and smells of the here and now.

With practice, mindfulness allows us to take a step back from our busy brains. It offers us the space to recognize negative thought patterns or the familiar scripts we repeat to ourselves. It gives us the clarity to acknowledge them and the ability to gently let them just be. Much like the weather ever changes, so do our emotions. Mindfulness teaches us to let them come and go, with no judgement, and to focus more on the present moment.

AFFIRMATION OF THE MONTH

I will gently welcome mindfulness into everything I do

JUN 27 – JUL 3
Mindfulness

27 / MONDAY	28 / TUESDAY	29 / WEDNESDAY ●

NOTES

> "Walk with awareness. Eat with awareness. Breathe with awareness"
>
> OSHO (1931–1990), INDIAN GURU

30 / THURSDAY

_____

_____

_____

_____

_____

_____

_____

_____

_____

_____

1 / FRIDAY
Canada Day

_____

_____

_____

_____

_____

_____

_____

_____

_____

2 / SATURDAY

_____

_____

_____

3 / SUNDAY

_____

_____

_____

_____

GIVE YOUR FULL ATTENTION

With technology it's easy to be permanently distracted and never fully engaged. We watch TV whilst scrolling Instagram; have lunch whilst checking emails. This week, spend quality time with someone. Turn off all distractions and really listen and engage with them. Notice the little things, and try to be fully present.

JUL 4 – JUL 10
mindfulness

4 / MONDAY
Independence Day (USA)

5 / TUESDAY

6 / WEDNESDAY

NOTES

> "All that we are is the result of what we have thought. The mind is everything. What we think we become"
>
> GAUTAMA BUDDHA (c. 563–483BCE)

7 / THURSDAY ☽

_____

_____

_____

_____

_____

_____

_____

_____

_____

_____

8 / FRIDAY

_____

_____

_____

_____

_____

_____

_____

_____

_____

_____

9 / SATURDAY

Eid al-Adha (Feast of the Sacrifice) begins at sundown

_____

_____

_____

_____

10 / SUNDAY

_____

_____

_____

_____

_____

_____

LIKE THE WEATHER

Feelings are a part of life and with the good there is also the bad. It can be so easy to get caught up and controlled by your feelings. Try to think of them as the weather. Let them come, feel what you need to feel but trust that they will eventually pass. Storms do not last forever, there is always sunshine on the way.

JUL 11 – JUL 17
mindfulness

11 / MONDAY

12 / TUESDAY
Orangemen's Day (NIR)

13 / WEDNESDAY ○

NOTES

> # "Nothing can bring you peace but yourself"
> RALPH WALDO EMERSON (1803–1882), AMERICAN WRITER

14 / THURSDAY
Bastille Day

_____
_____
_____
_____
_____
_____
_____
_____
_____
_____

15 / FRIDAY

_____
_____
_____
_____
_____
_____
_____
_____
_____
_____

16 / SATURDAY

_____
_____
_____

17 / SUNDAY

_____
_____
_____
_____
_____
_____

TAKE A MINDFUL SHOWER

Focusing on our senses is a wonderful way to guide our mind to the present. This week, when you shower, try to be aware of the thoughts and sensations that arise. Feel the water as it falls on your skin. How is the temperature? Go slowly, notice and savour each feeling, refocusing your mind to these sensations if it wanders.

JUL 18 – JUL 24
mindfulness

18 / MONDAY	19 / TUESDAY	20 / WEDNESDAY ☾

NOTES

> ## "It is the mind that makes the body"
> SOJOURNER TRUTH (*c.* 1797–1883), AMERICAN ACTIVIST

21 / THURSDAY

22 / FRIDAY

23 / SATURDAY ♌

----

24 / SUNDAY

JUST BREATHE

Being mindful of our bodies is so important. Often, we can tense up and alter our breathing without realizing. Stop. Take this moment to unclench your jaw. Drop your shoulders. Flatten your hands. Take a big breath. Try to be aware of any tensions that keep arising and gently practise this exercise when they do.

JUL 25 – JUL 31
Mindfulness

25 / MONDAY	26 / TUESDAY	27 / WEDNESDAY

NOTES

> "Those who cannot change their minds cannot change anything"
>
> GEORGE BERNARD SHAW (1856–1950), IRISH PLAYWRIGHT

28 / THURSDAY ●

_____
_____
_____
_____
_____
_____
_____
_____
_____
_____

29 / FRIDAY

Islamic New Year (first day
of Muharram) begins at
sundown

_____
_____
_____
_____
_____
_____
_____
_____
_____
_____

30 / SATURDAY

_____
_____
_____

31 / SUNDAY

_____
_____
_____
_____
_____

BE MINDFUL OF YOUR INNER VOICE

We live with our inner voice every day, so it is
important to be mindful of what it is saying.
This week, when a negative thought creeps in,
question it by asking: Is this helpful? Is it kind?
Would I say it to a friend? If the answer is no, it's
not something you should be saying to yourself,
or maybe there's a kinder way of saying it.

JULY OVERVIEW

M	TU	W	TH	F	SA	SU
27	28	29	30	1	2	3
4	5	6	7	8	9	10
11	12	13	14	15	16	17
18	19	20	21	22	23	24
25	26	27	28	29	30	31

this month I am grateful for . . .

_____

_____

_____

_____

_____

_____

_____

REFLECTIONS ON MINDFULNESS

Have you felt the benefits of practising some mindfulness this month?

_____

_____

_____

_____

_____

Are there any barriers that you feel hinder you and your practice of mindfulness? Can these be worked on?

_____

_____

_____

_____

_____

Are there any ways that you would like to develop mindfulness for the future?

_____

_____

_____

_____

AUGUST

JOY

It is often said, when life gives you lemons make lemonade. If only human emotions were this simple. Without feeling and processing the not-so-good parts of life, we can never healthily enjoy the good parts. As you heal and begin to move forwards, it's important to remember that joy is still there and always will be.

Joy is so often viewed as some elusive thing that we need to find. We can spend our lives chasing it, which in turn can lead us to feeling like we never really have it at all. However, there is joy to be found in most places, no matter how small. It can be the taste of that first sip of coffee in the morning. The weight of your cat sleeping soundly on your lap. The sound of a friend's laugh in a voice note. Joy is always there, longing to be found. Sometimes we just need to work on grounding ourselves and tuning into it more.

AFFIRMATION OF THE MONTH

I will lean into every moment of joy, no matter how small

AUG 1 – AUG 7

JOY

1 / MONDAY
August Bank Holiday (ROI, SCO)
Public Holiday (NSW, NT)
Lughnasadh (Lammas)

_____
_____
_____
_____
_____
_____
_____
_____
_____
_____

2 / TUESDAY

_____
_____
_____
_____
_____
_____
_____
_____
_____
_____
_____

3 / WEDNESDAY

_____
_____
_____
_____
_____
_____
_____
_____
_____
_____
_____

NOTES

_____
_____
_____

"A day without laughter is a day wasted"

CHARLIE CHAPLIN (1889–1977), ENGLISH ACTOR

4 / THURSDAY

5 / FRIDAY ☽

6 / SATURDAY

7 / SUNDAY

THIS IS PURE HAPPINESS

It is important to recognize what fills us up and brings us joy. It allows us to focus on what we really care about, and hopefully means we can seek these moments out more! Write down three things that bring you true happiness. Leave them somewhere you can see them, as a regular reminder of the joy they bring.

AUG 8 – AUG 14

JOY

8 / MONDAY

9 / TUESDAY

10 / WEDNESDAY

NOTES

> *"Whoever is happy will make others happy too"*
>
> ANNE FRANK (1929–1945), GERMAN DIARIST

11 / THURSDAY

---

12 / FRIDAY ○

---

13 / SATURDAY

---

14 / SUNDAY

LAUGHTER IS A TONIC

Nothing beats a good belly laugh. Laughter connects us with others and eases stress. This week, try to seek out something that really tickles you. Whether it be a phone call with a friend who makes you howl, a TV show or a few funny YouTube videos. Laughter is joyous and you can never have too much.

AUG 15 – AUG 21

JOY

15 / MONDAY

16 / TUESDAY

17 / WEDNESDAY

NOTES

> "True happiness comes from the joy of deeds well done, the zest of creating new things"

ANTOINE DE SAINT-EXUPÉRY (1900–1944), FRENCH WRITER

18 / THURSDAY

19 / FRIDAY ☾

20 / SATURDAY

21 / SUNDAY

WATCH YOUR FAVOURITE FILM

Allowing joy into your life is so necessary. Life can be filled with ups and downs, so cherishing the joyful bits is very important. This week, make time in your schedule to watch a favourite film that truly brings you joy. Better still, share it with a good friend. Savour the moment and really soak that happiness in.

AUG 22 – AUG 28

JOY

22 / MONDAY

23 / TUESDAY

24 / WEDNESDAY ♍

NOTES

> "Action may not always bring happiness,
> but there is no happiness without action"

BENJAMIN DISRAELI (1804–1881), BRITISH POLITICIAN

25 / THURSDAY

26 / FRIDAY

27 / SATURDAY ●

28 / SUNDAY

WHEN WERE YOU HAPPIEST?

This week, think back over the past year.
When did you feel most happy? Why do you
think that is? If you can pinpoint what exactly
sparked your happiness, you can try to plan
more of that in your life. Making conscious
space for feeling that joy again means you
will always have it to look forward to.

AUGUST OVERVIEW

M	TU	W	TH	F	SA	SU
1	2	3	4	5	6	7
8	9	10	11	12	13	14
15	16	17	18	19	20	21
22	23	24	25	26	27	28
29	30	31	1	2	3	4

this month I am grateful for . . .

_____

_____

_____

_____

_____

_____

_____

REFLECTIONS ON JOY

Have you felt or been more aware of joy this month? In what ways?

_____

_____

_____

_____

_____

How did it feel to focus more on joy and to practise being more open to it?

_____

_____

_____

_____

_____

In what ways would you like to add more joy into your future? How can you do this?

_____

_____

_____

_____

_____

SEPTEMBER

EMPATHY

Many are born with the gift of being naturally empathetic, but it is also possible to learn how to feel more empathy, if it doesn't come naturally to you. To be able to feel empathy is a superpower. You are not only putting yourself in someone else's shoes, you are feeling the aches and pains of the path they've walked, and understanding it. Practising empathy allows people to feel less alone. It helps them to feel seen, heard and understood. It validates and holds space for their emotions, which in turn helps them to heal. In return it allows you to create a deeper connection with their emotions, which can broaden your whole outlook on life – and open your mind to things that are not within your experience.

AFFIRMATION OF THE MONTH

My empathy holds space for other people's feelings, and that is a wonderful gift

AUG 29 – SEP 4

Empathy

29 / MONDAY
Summer Bank Holiday (UK, except SCO)

_____
_____
_____
_____
_____
_____
_____
_____
_____
_____
_____
_____

30 / TUESDAY

_____
_____
_____
_____
_____
_____
_____
_____
_____
_____
_____
_____

31 / WEDNESDAY

_____
_____
_____
_____
_____
_____
_____
_____
_____
_____
_____
_____

NOTES

_____
_____
_____
_____

> "I do not ask the wounded person how he feels,
> I myself become the wounded person"

WALT WHITMAN (1819–1892), AMERICAN WRITER

1 / THURSDAY

_____
_____
_____
_____
_____
_____
_____
_____

2 / FRIDAY

_____
_____
_____
_____
_____
_____
_____
_____

3 / SATURDAY ☽

_____
_____
_____

4 / SUNDAY
Father's Day (AUS, NZ)

_____
_____
_____
_____

SAY THANK YOU

Think about a time someone has shown
empathy towards you. How did it make you
feel? Write a letter or message to that person
thanking them for showing you the empathy
you needed and explaining why it helped.
There is no need to send it if you don't feel
comfortable doing so; it can just be for you.

SEP 5 – SEP 11

Empathy

5 / MONDAY
Labor Day (CAN, USA)

6 / TUESDAY

7 / WEDNESDAY

NOTES

> "Reading is equivalent to thinking with someone else's head instead of with one's own"

ARTHUR SCHOPENHAUER (1788–1860), GERMAN PHILOSOPHER

8 / THURSDAY

9 / FRIDAY

10 / SATURDAY ○

---

11 / SUNDAY

SPEND SOME TIME WITH OTHERS

People who spend time with individuals who are very different to themselves tend to develop a more empathetic outlook towards others. Take a moment to think about if you could broaden your circle to interact with others with a different worldview to you. Do you feel this would increase your empathy?

SEP 12 – SEP 18

empathy

12 / MONDAY	13 / TUESDAY	14 / WEDNESDAY

NOTES

"None knows the weight of another's burden"

GEORGE HERBERT (1593–1633), WELSH POET

15 / THURSDAY

16 / FRIDAY

17 / SATURDAY ☾

18 / SUNDAY

CONTACT A FRIEND WHO'S HURTING

Empathy is the ability to imagine ourselves in someone else's situation and see their perspective. Think of someone you know who might be struggling or having a hard time. Send a message or call them to let them know you're thinking of them. That little gesture could make a world of difference.

SEP 19 – SEP 25
Empathy

19 / MONDAY

20 / TUESDAY

21 / WEDNESDAY
International Day of Peace

NOTES

"The more a man knows, the more he forgives"

CATHERINE THE GREAT (1729–1796), RUSSIAN EMPRESS

22 / THURSDAY

_____

_____

_____

_____

_____

_____

_____

_____

_____

_____

_____

23 / FRIDAY
Autumn Equinox (UK, ROI, CAN, USA)
Spring Equinox (AUS, NZ)

_____

_____

_____

_____

_____

_____

_____

_____

_____

_____

_____

24 / SATURDAY ♎

_____

_____

_____

_____

25 / SUNDAY ●
Rosh Hashanah (Jewish New Year) begins at sundown

_____

_____

_____

_____

_____

TAKE SOME TIME OUT

Do you consider yourself an empath? Being an empath can be hard; you not only understand others' emotions, but feel it with them. This excess of emotions can lead to an empathy overload. If you have experienced this, how could you help to ease your own emotions? Are there some boundaries you could put in place?

SEPTEMBER OVERVIEW

M	TU	W	TH	F	SA	SU
29	30	31	1	2	3	4
5	6	7	8	9	10	11
12	13	14	15	16	17	18
19	20	21	22	23	24	25
26	27	28	29	30	1	2

this month I am grateful for . . .

_____

_____

_____

_____

_____

_____

REFLECTIONS ON EMPATHY

Has focusing on empathy this month affected you in any way? How?

_____

_____

_____

_____

_____

How does it feel when someone else shows you empathy?

_____

_____

_____

_____

_____

In what ways do you think empathy could help you in the future?

_____

_____

_____

_____

_____

OCTOBER

CREATIVITY

People often assume creativity is just for those with a talent for the arts, but we are all creative, every day. The key is to notice your own creativity. Whether it's cooking up a new meal in the kitchen or settling in with a cup of tea and colouring book on an evening. It could even be creating ideas through a well-nourished imagination, or tangible creations through arts, craft or music. Creativity is a constant and can provide us with so much pleasure and fulfilment. You do not have to be naturally talented or "gifted" to enjoy the benefits of it. Having a particular creative outlet can help enormously in reducing stress and anxiety. It can be a safe place to tackle your thoughts and feelings and be incredibly therapeutic. Use this month's prompts to help you find and encourage your creative side.

AFFIRMATION OF THE MONTH

I am creating a life I love and that works for me

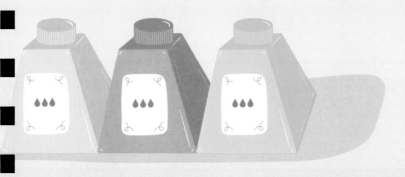

SEP 26 – OCT 2

creativity

26 / MONDAY
Public Holiday (WA)

27 / TUESDAY

28 / WEDNESDAY

NOTES

> "Creativity is not the finding of a thing, but the making something out of it after it is found"

JAMES RUSSELL LOWELL (1819–1891), AMERICAN POET

29 / THURSDAY

30 / FRIDAY

1 / SATURDAY
Black History Month begins (UK)

2 / SUNDAY

CHANNEL YOUR INNER CHILD

As children we are at our most creative, and least inhibited or worried about "getting it wrong". Think of something you loved to do as a child. Was it painting, playing with modelling clay, baking, singing? Spend a bit of time this week connecting with your inner child and indulging your past childhood creative passions.

OCT 3 – OCT 9

creativity

3 / MONDAY ☽
Public Holiday (ACT, NSW, QLD, SA)

4 / TUESDAY
Yom Kippur (Day of Atonement) begins at sundown

5 / WEDNESDAY

NOTES

> "Every child is an artist. The problem is how to remain an artist once we grow up"
>
> PABLO PICASSO (188–1973), SPANISH ARTIST

6 / THURSDAY

_____

_____

_____

_____

_____

_____

_____

_____

_____

_____

7 / FRIDAY

Milad un-Nabi (Sunni; birthday of the Prophet Muhammad) begins at sundown

_____

_____

_____

_____

_____

_____

_____

_____

_____

8 / SATURDAY

_____

_____

_____

_____

9 / SUNDAY ○

Sukkot (Feast of the Tabernacles) begins at sundown

_____

_____

_____

_____

COOK SOMETHING CREATIVE

We can easily get stuck in ruts when walking through life. This often leads to us repeating the same things for the habit, comfort and ease of it. This week, instead of cooking the same meals, try something completely new. Not a fan of cooking? Visit a café or restaurant and pick a wildcard meal from the menu!

OCT 10 – OCT 16

creativity

10 / MONDAY
Thanksgiving (CAN)
Indigenous Peoples' Day/
Columbus Day

11 / TUESDAY

12 / WEDNESDAY

NOTES

> "The power of imagination makes us infinite"

JOHN MUIR (1838–1914), SCOTTISH-AMERICAN NATURALIST

13 / THURSDAY

14 / FRIDAY

15 / SATURDAY

_____
_____
_____
_____
_____
_____

16 / SUNDAY

_____
_____
_____
_____
_____

CREATE TIME FOR YOU

Have you always wanted to try a new hobby or get out of your usual routine? Even if just for a few minutes this week, try to create a little bit of time when you can do just that. Whether it's practising the piano or simply putting aside ten minutes to read a chapter of your book, make sure to create that important time for you.

OCT 17 – OCT 23

creativity

17 / MONDAY ☾

18 / TUESDAY

19 / WEDNESDAY

NOTES

"Creativity takes courage"

HENRI MATISSE (1869–1954), FRENCH ARTIST

20 / THURSDAY　　　**21 / FRIDAY**　　　**22 / SATURDAY**

_____　　_____　　_____
_____　　_____　　_____
_____　　_____　　_____
_____　　_____　　_____
_____　　_____　　_____

23 / SUNDAY

_____　　_____　　_____
_____　　_____　　_____
_____　　_____　　_____
_____　　_____　　_____

CATHARTIC CREATIVITY

Sometimes we can get the same sense of
fulfillment from other people's creativity.
This week, immerse yourself in someone else's
creative soul. Whether it be visiting an art
gallery, going to a concert or reading some
poetry. Sometimes other people can put into
words what we struggle to articulate and help
us feel emotions we have been searching for.

creativity

24 / MONDAY ♏
Diwali
Labour Day (NZ)

25 / TUESDAY ●

26 / WEDNESDAY

NOTES

> "Imagination is the only weapon in
> the war against reality"

LEWIS CARROLL (1832–1898), ENGLISH AUTHOR

27 / THURSDAY

28 / FRIDAY

29 / SATURDAY

30 / SUNDAY
British Summer Time ends

CREATE NEW SKILLS

Have you always said you want to travel more?
Start a dance class? Learn a language? This
week, compose a list of these creative desires.
Set an intention to try out the things you
have always meant to do, planning exactly
how you will find time/money/space to do so.
How could you make these dreams a reality?

OCTOBER OVERVIEW

M	TU	W	TH	F	SA	SU
26	27	28	29	30	1	2
3	4	5	6	7	8	9
10	11	12	13	14	15	16
17	18	19	20	21	22	23
24	25	26	27	28	29	30
31	1	2	3	4	5	6

this month I am grateful for . . .

_____

_____

_____

_____

_____

_____

REFLECTIONS ON CREATIVITY

How have you practised being more creative this month?

_____

_____

_____

_____

_____

_____

How has it made you feel?

_____

_____

_____

_____

_____

_____

Would you like to continue being creative in the future? How can you make this happen?

_____

_____

_____

_____

_____

Don't miss out on next year's diary! See the back page for details on how to order your copy

NOVEMBER

AUTHENTICITY

To show up authentically as our honest inner selves can feel like a scary and vulnerable thing to do, but it can also be the most liberating act of self-kindness.

There is no comfort in restricting, bending or moulding ourselves into something else, just so we can fit in. There is no peace in knowing we are suppressing our own soul to feel like we "belong". By being honest with ourselves and staying true to our sense of self, we open up to a genuine existence that ultimately is not only more fulfilling but also more enjoyable. Making the decision to live your life authentically to you is like coming home to yourself.

Use the prompts over the coming month to help you find and nourish your true authentic self.

AFFIRMATION OF THE MONTH

I will be true to my own heart and fully embrace my beautiful soul

OCT 31 – NOV 6
Authenticity

31 / MONDAY
Halloween
Samhain
October Bank Holiday
(ROI)

1 / TUESDAY ☽
All Saints' Day

2 / WEDNESDAY
All Souls' Day

NOTES

"Be yourself. Everyone else is already taken"

OSCAR WILDE (1854–1900), IRISH POET AND PLAYWRIGHT

3 / THURSDAY

4 / FRIDAY

5 / SATURDAY

6 / SUNDAY
Daylight Saving Time ends
(CAN, USA)

BE TRUE TO YOU

Sometimes other people's expectations of us
can hold us back from being our true authentic
souls. Write a list of how you feel pigeon-holed,
limited or held back by others' views of you.
Can you implement a gentle action of change
to break free from generalizations? Notice how
this makes you feel more confident and free.

NOV 7 – NOV 13
Authenticity

7 / MONDAY	8 / TUESDAY ○	9 / WEDNESDAY

NOTES

> ## "To believe in something, and not to live it, is dishonest"
>
> MAHATMA GANDHI (1869–1948), INDIAN LAWYER AND ACTIVIST

10 / THURSDAY

_____

_____

_____

_____

_____

_____

_____

_____

11 / FRIDAY
Veterans Day (USA)
Remembrance Day (CAN)

_____

_____

_____

_____

_____

_____

_____

_____

12 / SATURDAY

_____

_____

_____

13 / SUNDAY
Remembrance Sunday (UK)

_____

_____

_____

_____

OPTIMIZE YOUR SCHEDULE

To be true to ourselves means being honest about what does (and doesn't) bring us joy. Think about the commitments you've taken on. Do they all bring you joy? Choose one thing that doesn't feel authentic to you and politely say no to it. Plan how you can use this time for something that brings you genuine fulfillment.

NOV 14 – NOV 20
Authenticity

14 / MONDAY

15 / TUESDAY

16 / WEDNESDAY ☾

NOTES

"Knowing yourself is the beginning of all wisdom"

ARISTOTLE (384–322BCE), GREEK PHILOSOPHER

17 / THURSDAY

_____
_____
_____
_____
_____
_____

18 / FRIDAY

_____
_____
_____
_____
_____
_____

19 / SATURDAY

_____
_____
_____
_____

20 / SUNDAY

_____
_____
_____
_____

UNAPOLOGETICALLY YOU

It is important to surround ourselves with people who bring out the best in us. The people who allow us to be our most whole and real self. Think about who these people are for you, and make sure they know how much you appreciate them. Can you quietly and gently distance yourself from people who are not on that list?

NOV 21 – NOV 27
Authenticity

21 / MONDAY
World Hello Day

22 / TUESDAY

23 / WEDNESDAY ♐ ●

NOTES

> "We have to dare to be ourselves, however frightening or strange that self may prove to be"

MAY SARTON (1912–1995), AMERICAN-BELGIAN WRITER

24 / THURSDAY
Thanksgiving Day (USA)

25 / FRIDAY

26 / SATURDAY

27 / SUNDAY
First Sunday of Advent

SOCIAL MEDIA

Similarly to real life, it's important to ensure our social media is a safe and friendly space to be our full selves in. Spend an evening this week going through your feed and really think about whether the people you follow help or hinder you to be true to you. Unfollow, unfriend or even block anyone who does not.

NOVEMBER OVERVIEW

M	TU	W	TH	F	SA	SU
31	1	2	3	4	5	6
7	8	9	10	11	12	13
14	15	16	17	18	19	20
21	22	23	24	25	26	27
28	29	30	1	2	3	4

This month I am grateful for . . .

_____

_____

_____

_____

_____

_____

REFLECTIONS ON AUTHENTICITY

How have you sought a more authentic life this month?

_____

_____

_____

_____

_____

How has it felt to try to be truer to your deeply authentic self?

_____

_____

_____

_____

_____

Are there other areas of your life where you think being more authentic could be beneficial?

_____

_____

_____

_____

_____

DECEMBER

KINDNESS

The world can feel heavy and dark at times, and kindness can instantly ease this. Kindness is always a tonic. It has the ability to completely alter someone's day, change their perspective and make things softer and easier. Kindness can help people heal. Tackling conflict with kindness, rather than anger or annoyance, can help us to practise a deeper level of understanding to another person's plight. This in turn can completely reframe our own outlook on life. No matter how small, kindness makes a difference. So keep implementing the ripples of kindness everywhere you go, for yourself and for others, because sometimes even the smallest of ripples together can make a wave.

AFFIRMATION OF THE MONTH

I know that my kindness holds more power and weight than I ever thought possible

NOV 28 – DEC 4
kindness

28 / MONDAY

29 / TUESDAY

30 / WEDNESDAY ☽
St Andrew's Day

NOTES

> "Kind words can be short and easy to speak,
> but their echoes are truly endless"

MOTHER TERESA (1910–1997), CATHOLIC MISSIONARY

1 / THURSDAY
World AIDS Day

2 / FRIDAY

3 / SATURDAY

4 / SUNDAY

NOTES FOR A STRANGER

A small act of kindness can transform someone's day for the better. This week, leave a friendly note, a book, bunch of flowers or a handwritten poem in a public place for someone else to find. Discovering it might just give them a sense of human connection and offer the light they needed on a dark day.

DEC 5 – DEC 11
kindness

5 / MONDAY

6 / TUESDAY

7 / WEDNESDAY

NOTES

> ## "Three things ... are important: the first is to be kind; the second is to be kind; and the third is to be kind"
>
> HENRY JAMES (1843–1916), AMERICAN-BRITISH WRITER

8 / THURSDAY ○
Bodhi Day (Buddha's Enlightenment) in some countries

_____

_____

_____

_____

_____

_____

_____

_____

_____

_____

9 / FRIDAY

_____

_____

_____

_____

_____

_____

_____

_____

_____

_____

10 / SATURDAY

_____

_____

_____

11 / SUNDAY

_____

_____

_____

_____

_____

BE KIND TO YOURSELF

When was the last time you were actively kind to yourself? Compare how you speak to yourself with how you speak to loved ones. Practise speaking to yourself in a similar manner. This week, wake up and give yourself three compliments. The more you tell yourself kind things, the more you will believe them.

for you
xx

DEC 12 – DEC 18
kindness

12 / MONDAY	13 / TUESDAY	14 / WEDNESDAY

NOTES

> ## "Deliberately seek opportunities for kindness, sympathy and patience"
>
> EVELYN UNDERHILL (1875–1941), ENGLISH WRITER

15 / THURSDAY

16 / FRIDAY ☾

17 / SATURDAY

18 / SUNDAY
Hanukkah begins at sundown

OFFER A RANDOM COMPLIMENT

Words of kindness are powerful. This week, make an effort to compliment people more. If they are wearing a lovely shirt, tell them. When you receive good service, say so. If they have done something that made you joyful, let them know! Too often these things go unsaid. A small compliment can go such a long way.

for you
xx

DEC 19 – DEC 25
kindness

19 / MONDAY

20 / TUESDAY

21 / WEDNESDAY
Winter Solstice (UK, ROI, CAN, USA)

NOTES

> "In spite of everything, I still believe that people are really good at heart"

ANNE FRANK (1929–1945), GERMAN DIARIST

22 / THURSDAY ♑
Summer Solstice (AUS, NZ)

23 / FRIDAY ●

24 / SATURDAY
Christmas Eve

_____
_____
_____
_____
_____

25 / SUNDAY
Christmas Day

_____
_____
_____
_____

KINDNESS STARTS WITH YOU

Being kind to ourselves is so often a more difficult task than being kind to others. This week, turn to the "Inspired Journalling" section and make a list of all the things you love about yourself. It may feel awkward, but having them written down means you can go back to them and remind yourself when you need it most.

for
you
x x

DEC 26 – JAN 1
kindness

26 / MONDAY
Boxing Day / St Stephen's Day
Kwanzaa begins

27 / TUESDAY
Christmas Day (substitute holiday

28 / WEDNESDAY

NOTES

> ## "No act of kindness, no matter how small, is ever wasted"
>
> AESOP (c. 620–564BCE), GREEK STORYTELLER

29 / THURSDAY

30 / FRIDAY ☽

31 / SATURDAY
New Year's Eve

_____

1 / SUNDAY
New Year's Day
Kwanzaa ends

IT'S THE KINDNESS THAT COUNTS

Kindness doesn't always have to be big gestures. Often it's the smallest acts that make the biggest difference. It's taking an extra minute to listen, offering a helping hand or giving a reassuring hug. Think about who has shown you kindness this year. Spend five minutes writing them a few kind words to thank them for altering your world for the better.

for you
xx

DECEMBER OVERVIEW

M	TU	W	TH	F	SA	SU
28	29	30	1	2	3	4
5	6	7	8	9	10	11
12	13	14	15	16	17	18
19	20	21	22	23	24	25
26	27	28	29	30	31	1

This month I am grateful for . . .

_____

_____

_____

_____

_____

_____

REFLECTIONS ON KINDNESS

How have you brought more kindness into your life this month?

_____

_____

_____

_____

_____

How has focusing on kindness for yourself and others made you feel?

_____

_____

_____

_____

_____

How do you think you can implement more kindness into your life for the future?

_____

_____

_____

_____

_____

INSPIRED JOURNALLING

The journalling pages that follow will encourage you to spend a little time reflecting on some of the things that many people hold dear, which will hopefully inspire you to pursue some of your own goals as you move through the year.

Each of the six pages corresponds to one of the monthly themes in the main diary and gives you space to make a personalized list – of places you'd like to visit, things you love about yourself, self-care ideas, films and TV shows you'd like to watch, what gives you joy, and books you'd like to read.

Just write down as few or as many ideas as they come into your mind under each theme. And, remember, you can come back to these lists and add to them any time you want, and indeed continue them elsewhere if you'd like, so just use them as will best benefit you...

what am I Grateful for?

GRATITUDE (JANUARY)

Spending time reflecting on the things we are grateful for is a wonderful way to ground us when our thoughts are spiralling. In times of uncertainty it can offer us some sense of stability. It can set us up with a more positive mindset and aid us in our happiness. Honing in on what enhances our lives and fills us up emotionally can also offer us some insight into what we perhaps need to incorporate more of in our lives too.

Use the space below to compile a list of all the things you are grateful for. What makes you feel happy, whole and contented? What helps you feel fulfilled? What gives you purpose?

Refer back to the list whenever you need reminding of the good things in life.

self-care Ideas

RESILIENCE (MARCH)

The way we treat ourselves and how we speak to ourselves is so important. Recognizing when we need rest, care and time is integral to our emotional wellbeing. Knowing what we can do in these times of crisis and need is equally as important. When we are in the thick of it, it is sometimes difficult to remember what helps us and what aids our recharge and recovery. These are all key components for drawing on our resilience.

Use this page to write down all the things that fill you up, provide you with comfort and help you when you are having a difficult time. If you find it hard to think of a few specific things on the spot, keep coming back and adding to it when you've recognized something that has helped. Not only is it a great way of acknowledging your self-compassion, it will also become a wonderful resource when a really bad day arrives and your thoughts are more cloudy.

Films & Programmes I'd Like To Watch & Books I'd Like to Read

COMPASSION (APRIL)

Life can get busy and hectic, often quickly with no warning. Sometimes we can get so swept up in it we don't even realize how frazzled we're becoming. It's so easy to keep going and going, and forget to show ourselves some much-needed compassion. We all need time and space to take care and nourish our souls. A great way to take some time out and have some much-needed rest is to watch a good boxset, film or get lost in a good book.

Use the space below to make a list of all the TV, films or books you'd like to get lost in for a bit of down time and distance away from the hectic pace of life.

Letter to my younger self

GROWTH (MAY)

Growing up is full of ups and downs, trials and tribulations. We soak up so much and take so many of our childhood experiences into adulthood. With this in mind, when you think about your younger years is there a period of time that feels like a particularly significant phase of challenge, growth or transition for you?

Think yourself in this past moment and write yourself a letter. What would you have wanted to hear? What message of support can you offer? Not only will writing it possibly feel cathartic, but it will also highlight how much you have grown. It will show you how much your life experiences have shaped you and how you have become the version of yourself you are now.

what brings me joy?

JOY (AUGUST)

Knowing what lights us up, what makes us happy and what brings us joy is so important. With this knowledge we know where to place our priorities and energy. We know what to seek when times are tough and who the people and places are that fill us up with goodness. By concentrating on these things, by making more time for them and opening our lives to them more, we can create a more fulfilling and uplifting life for ourselves.

With this in mind, in this space write a list of things that bring you joy. The things, people and places that make you feel whole, seen, heard and happy. That bring out the best you that you can be. When you are lost, or struggling to find your way you can refer to this list to remind yourself what you perhaps need to make more room for in order to overcome it.

what do I like about me?

KINDNESS (DECEMBER)

Often our inner critic does a great job of pointing out our weak spots, honing in on the negative, and amplifying our perceived failures. Comparing ourselves too often to others can mean that all we see in others is good, compared to our "bad". Let's challenge that habit by offering ourselves some kindness.

Write down a list of all the things you love about yourself, and all the wonderful things you have achieved. If this feels challenging at first, perhaps ask a loved one or your best friend what they love most about you, and write that down. Create a "brag file" and write down all compliments and congratulations you receive, at work and in your personal life. Celebrate all your successes, however small you feel they are. Keep this list and often refer to it when you are feeling low on confidence.

Notes

Don't miss out on
next year's diary!

To pre-order your 2023 *Every Day Matters Diary*
with FREE postage and packing,*
call our UK distributor on +44 (0)1206 255800.

*Free postage and packing for UK delivery addresses only. Offer limited to 3 books per order.

WATKINS
Sharing Wisdom Since 1893

Our books celebrate conscious, passionate, wise and happy living.
Be part of the community by visiting
watkinspublishing.com

 WatkinsPublishing    @watkinswisdom
WatkinsPublishingLtd   +watkinspublishing1893